I0163880

Allen's Guide to Understanding and Appreciating Wines

By

Robert Allen Morris

Orchid Springs Publishing, LLC
329 N. Park Ave., Floor 2
Winter Park, FL 32789

Copyright© 2014 as the appendix to
The Wine Queen
All Rights Reserved
ISBN Paperback: 978-0-9960684-5-1
ISBN EBook: 978-0-9960684-7-5

Contents

Introduction

There are 58 countries in the world that produced 6.8 billion gallons of wine in 2012, but Italy, France, Spain and the U.S. account for over half of world wine production (*The Wine Institute*). The U.S. is the largest wine market in the world, with France and Italy ranking second and third. California is the fourth leading wine producer in the world, behind Italy, France and Spain, and produces 90 percent of the wine produced in the U.S. Other states that produce wine, in order of amount produced, include Washington, New York, Oregon, Texas and others (*Wines & Vines*). There are 4,600 wine grape growers in California that in 2013 harvested 4.2 million tons of wine grapes from seventeen grape growing districts, that was produced into 662.8 million gallons of wine (*California Grape Crush Report 2013, California Association of Wine Grape Growers*). California's $61.5 billion wine industry employs 330,000 people and produces wine grapes on 526,000 acres crushed in 3,754 wineries. Because of California's dominance in wine production, and the fact that its varieties of grapes and the types of its wines are the same as those of the other dominant wine producers in the world, this report will focus on California wines.

The remainder of this book is organized into three sections. *Viticulture* describes how grapes are produced, wine grape varieties, what determines quality in grapes and wine, and pest and diseases that can affect vineyards. *Enology* is a step-by-step description of the wine making process, from crushing the grapes, through the fermentation process, to aging the wines. Making table wines, Champagnes and dessert wines are described. *Tasting Wines* describes the four major components that make up the taste of wine, the five stages of wine tasting, and how to evaluate wine quality. Matching wines with foods is also covered.

Viticulture

It all starts with grape growing, called viticulture. Viticulture, from the Latin word for *vine,* is the science, production, and study of grapes, which deals with the series of events that occur in the vineyard. The quality of any wine is dictated by the quality of the grapes it is made from. The seventeen grape growing districts in California can be grouped into three regions according to grape quality. The three regions are the Central Valley, which encompasses all or parts of nineteen counties and includes the San Joaquin and Sacramento Valleys where Madera, Modesto, Fresno, Sacramento, and Visalia are located; the North Coast which is four counties north of San Francisco - Lake, Marin, Mendocino, and Solano; and the Napa Valley, which is Napa and Sonoma counties. The Central Valley is where the lowest quality wine grapes come from. Most wines made from these grapes are used in blends for generic wines. They also produce a lot of Thompson seedless grapes for raisins. The North Coast counties are the next step up in quality, and where a number of varietal wines are produced. The Napa Valley has the highest quality wine grapes. Grape prices and yields per acre in each of these regions vary greatly because they reflect the quality of the grapes.

Duties of the viticulturist include: monitoring and controlling pests and diseases with sprays, fertilization, irrigation, weed control, canopy management, monitoring fruit development and characteristics, vine pruning during the winter months, replanting vines lost to disease, and deciding when to harvest. Viticulturists are often intimately involved with winemakers, because vineyard management and the resulting grape characteristics provide the basis from which winemaking begins.

Vitis Vinifera is the species of grape used to make wine in California and Wine grape prices differ by region and grape variety. In 2013, all varieties of wine grapes averaged $383 per ton in the Central Valley, $1,162 per ton in the North Coast Counties, and $2,960 per ton in the Napa Valley. In the Napa Valley, Chardonnay grapes were $2,469 per ton while Gewurztraminer was $1,400, and Cabernet Sauvignon was $5,474 compared to Merlot at $2,771 per ton. These prices will fluctuate from year-to-year with fluctuating supplies.

Grape yields also vary by region. In the Napa Valley, average yields are two to four tons per acre, in the North Coast Counties, it's about five to seven, and in the San Joaquin Valley, growers get ten to twelve tons per acre. Other than geographical region, vine spacing and density per acre, pruning, soil fertility, altitude, temperature, management practices, and grape variety are most of the things that affect yield. Generally low yields, if they are the desired result of pruning and/or management practices, produce better quality wine because more of the vine's nutrients are directed into fewer grapes. The winemaker usually works with the vineyard manager to style the grapes, by pruning and other management practices, to make the grapes he wants for his wines.

About 120 gallons of wine is produced per ton in the Napa Valley and about 150-170 gallons per ton is produced in the other grape growing regions of California. Wine yields are lower in the Napa Valley because some of the same variables that affect grape yields also affect wine yields. These include differences in temperatures, altitude, amount of rainfall and irrigation, pruning practices, and vineyard management practices. How hard the grapes are pressed when making wine also affects wine yields.

Europe. In the northeastern US, primarily upper New York State, *Vitis Labrusca,* a species native to America, predominates as the species of grape, primarily Concord, Catawba, and Niagara, used to make wine. There are also French hybrids, which are derived from crosses between *Vitis Vinifera* and a number of American species, but mostly *Vitis Labrusca. Vitis Rotundifolia,* a species native the Eastern United States, is believed to have originated in North Carolina. Two varieties of grapes are produced from *Vitis Rotundifolia,* the Scuppernong, a white grape, colored light greenish brown, and the Muscadine a deep purple grape. They grow from New York State to Florida, and wines have been made from them since the sixteenth century. They are typically sweet dessert wines. The Scuppernong and Muscadine are also popular for fresh consumption.

Varietal wines carry the name of the grape they are produced from while generic wines carry the name of a wine producing region, usually somewhere in France. Varietal wines must derive at least 75% of their volume from the grape variety designated on the label. California generic wines are a blend of several varieties, usually of low-cost grapes from the Central Valley. White generics, sometimes called jug wines, include Chablis and Rhine wine, and red generics include Bordeaux and Burgundy. There are also Rose wines, pink wines made from red grapes. According to the 2013 California Grape Crush Report, there are 46 varieties of white wine grapes and 74 red varieties. The most popular for red varietals are

5

Cabernet Sauvignon, Pinot Noir, Petite Syrah and Zinfandel, and Chardonnay, Gewurztraminer, Johannisberg Riesling, and Chenin Blanc for white varietals.

The main varieties used in generic white wines are Thompson seedless, French Colombard, Sauvignon Blanc, Chenin Blanc and Gray Riesling. Zinfandel, Merlot, Gamay Beaujolais, Barbera and Petite Syrah are the main varieties used for generic red wines. Prior to the 1980s, generic wines were 85-90 percent of the wines consumed in the U.S. Now generics are 44 percent of wines consumed in the U.S., while varietals and premium generics are 54 percent.

The Vitis Vinifera wine grapes grown in California and Europe require deep, well-drained soils, at least five feet, but deeper is better. It takes three years after planting for the vines to produce a harvestable crop, and from 5 years (Central Valley) to 10 years (Napa valley) before they are in full production. On average, the vines have about a thirty year life, although there are vineyards in California that are eighty years old. Pruning cuts the vine back so there is new growth. If the vine wasn't pruned, it would soon produce so many grapes it would die.

The vine needs approximately thirteen to fifteen hundred hours of sunshine during the growing season and around twenty-seven inches of rainfall throughout the year in order to produce grapes suitable for winemaking. In ideal circumstances, the vine will receive most of the rainfall during the winter and spring months. Rain at harvest time can create many hazards, such as fungal diseases and berry splitting. The optimum weather during the growing season is a long, warm summer that allows the grapes the opportunity to ripen fully and to develop a balance between the levels of acids and sugars in the grape.

Topography is important, too. Hillsides and slopes are preferred over flatter terrain. Vines growing on a slope receive a greater strength of the sun's rays with sunshine falling on an angle perpendicular to the hillside. In flatter terrain, the strength of the sunlight is diluted as it is spread out across a wider surface area. Additionally, a slope affords better drainage, obviating the possibility that the vine might sit in overly moist soil. In cooler regions of the northern hemisphere, south-facing slopes receive more hours of sunlight and are preferred; in warmer climates, north-facing slopes are preferred.

Microclimates, which also affect grape quality, are climates that differ in various spots that may range from a hundred yards apart to a mile or more. They differ as a result of air currents and temperature changes from day to night. Air drainage from canyons in mountains over a particular area often creates a microclimate. These make wines different even though the vineyards the grapes came from may be less than a mile apart.

Major threats to vineyards are primarily adverse weather, diseases, and plant viruses. Frost from cold weather is a hazard in the Napa Valley sometimes. Frost is the solid deposition of water vapor from saturated air. It is formed when solid surfaces are cooled to below the dew point of the adjacent air as well as below the freezing point of water, about twenty-eight degrees. Sizes of frost crystals differ depending on time and water vapor available. Frost is also usually translucent in appearance. There are many types of frost, such as radiation and window frost. Frost causes economic damage when it destroys plants or hanging fruits. When the vine is flowering it is very susceptible to weather hazards such as strong winds and hail. Cold temperatures during this period can also bring the onset of millerandage, which produces clusters with no seeds and varying sizes. Too much heat can have the opposite affect and produce coulure, which causes grape clusters to either drop to the ground or not fully develop.

The main viticultural diseases include oidium, downy mildew, phylloxera, and plant viruses. Oidium is a fungus that causes powdery mildew on grape vines. It is a common pathogen of the wine grape. Infected plants display white powdery spots on the leaves and stems. The fungus is believed to have originated in North America. Oidium infects all green tissue on the grapevine, including leaves and young berries. It can cause crop loss and poor wine quality if untreated. This mildew can be treated with sulfur or fungicides. The initial symptoms of downy mildew appear on leaves as light to yellow spots. Infected vines become stunted with thick clusters of pale curled leaves. Severely infected leaves may drop from the vine. Infected immature grapes turn from green to light brown to purple and fall off the vine. Downy mildew is caused by a fungus called plasmopora uiticola. It is spread by wind driven rain. Control includes not planting susceptible cultivars, not planting vineyards in low or shady areas, and the use of fungicides. Grape phylloxera is a pest of commercial grapevines worldwide, originally native to eastern North America. These almost microscopic, pale yellow sap-sucking insects feed on the roots and leaves of grapevines depending on the phylloxera genetic strain. The resulting deformations on roots and secondary fungal infections can girdle roots, gradually cutting off the flow of nutrients and water to the vine, killing it.

In the nineteenth century, a phylloxera epidemic destroyed most of the vineyards for wine grapes in Europe, most notably in France. Phylloxera was introduced to Europe when avid botanists in Victorian England collected specimens of American vines in the 1850s. Because phylloxera is native to North America, the native grape species here are at least partially resistant. By contrast, the European wine grape is very susceptible to the insect. The epidemic devastated vineyards in Britain and then moved to the mainland, destroying most of the European wine growing industry. In 1863, the first vines began to deteriorate inexplicably in the southern Rhône region of France. The problem spread rapidly across the continent. In France alone, total wine production fell from eighty-four and a half million hectolitres in 1875 to only twenty-three-point-four million hectolitres in 1889. Some estimates hold that between two-thirds and nine-tenths of all European vineyards were destroyed.

Two major solutions gradually emerged: grafting cuttings onto resistant rootstocks and hybridization. Use of a resistant, or tolerant, rootstock involved grafting a Vitis Vinifera scion onto the roots of a resistant American native species. California viticulturists believe that American rootstocks saved the European wine industry. In France, the view is that those American vines that were taken to Europe in the 1850s caused the problem. Phylloxera also destroyed a lot of vineyards in California in the early twentieth century. It was gotten under control the same way as in Europe, by the use of a resistant or tolerant rootstock and grafting a Vitis Vinifera Scion onto the roots of an American native species. The rootstock does not interfere with the development of the wine grapes, and it furthermore allows the customization of the rootstock to soil and weather conditions, as well as desired vigor. Unfortunately, not all rootstocks are equally resistant. Modern phylloxera infestation also occurs when wineries are in need of fruit immediately, and choose to plant un-grafted vines rather than wait for grafted vines to be available.

Plant viruses are intracellular parasites that need a host to replicate. Plant-to-plant transmission usually involves vectors such as insects. Viruses are very small and can only be observed through a microscope. Viruses of concern limit the plant's ability to absorb nutrients, killing it. Key viruses to grape vines include leaf roll, corky bark and fan leaf.

Enology

The science and art of enology, or winemaking, has its roots in prehistoric times. The effects of alcohol were probably discovered when rotten fruit was consumed and found to have an intoxicating effect, which was viewed as pleasant. Fermented liquid could be stored for a long time without fear of decomposition, thus giving a reliable drinking source as well as a source of calories. Winemaking is believed to have begun about five thousand years ago in the Mediterranean basin. The first winemakers in California were the Franciscian Fathers, who founded a string of missions from San Diego to Sonoma that grew grapes and made wine, the last in 1823. Commercial grape growing and winemaking began in California in the 1830s. Phylloxera followed by prohibition pretty much destroyed the California wine industry, although a few wineries survived by making wines for religious occasions or by innovatively selling bricks of crushed grapes with specific instructions about what not to do to make wine. It was after World War II before California's wine industry really began again. The University of California at Davis can be credited for its many contributions to viticulture and enology. Shortly after the war, it developed and published standards for grape growing and winemaking that have helped make California wines as good as they are.

California can actually make better wines than Europe. California's climate is steadier than in France, Italy, or Spain. They have about two good winemaking years in ten. California only has about one year in ten or fifteen that isn't excellent.

Harvest is in many ways the first step in wine production. Grapes are harvested by hand. The decision to harvest grapes is typically made by the winemaker based on the level of brix, or sugar, and brix-to-acid ratio in the grapes. Harvest dates vary a little from year to year, but harvest in the Napa Valley is mostly in September and October. Most winemakers like a brix between twenty- and twenty-four, which is twenty- to twenty-four percent sugar content. Other considerations include ripeness, berry flavor, and tannin development, which are determined by skin color, seed color and taste. Overall disposition of the grapevine and weather forecasts are also taken into account.

Up until about 50 years ago, wine grapes were picked into fifty-pound wooden field boxes and loaded onto flat-bed trucks for transport to the winery. Now most grapes are picked into small metal tubs that each hold about forty pounds. These are lower in cost than wooden field boxes. When full, the tubs are dumped into larger bins holding about a thousand pounds of grapes on a trailer pulled by a tractor which follows the harvesting crews down the rows. Each of these harvesting bins is monitored by two people, who sift through the arriving grapes and pull out any unwanted material such as weeds, grape leaves, tree frogs, and so forth. The tractor dumps these bins into one to two ton detachable tanks, or three to five ton mounted tanks.

The use of knowledgeable harvesting labor costs more, but it pays for itself by enabling leaving behind the clusters that contain bunch rot or other defects. This can be an effective first line of defense to prevent inferior quality fruit from contaminating a lot or tank of wine.

After being hand harvested and loaded into detachable tanks, the grapes are taken into the winery and prepared for primary fermentation. De-stemming is the process of separating stems from the grapes. Depending on the winemaking procedure, this process may be undertaken before crushing with the purpose of lowering the development of tannins and vegetal flavors in the resulting wine, or after crushing to let those tannins develop.

Once the grapes have been transported to the winery, certain preparatory steps must be taken before the actual winemaking can begin. Cleanliness and sanitation are essential for good winemaking, as troublesome bacteria can cause disastrous results. Equipment must be sanitized with caustic soda, rinsed with water, and finally, treated with an anti-bacterial sulfite solution. To rid the equipment of excess sulfite, everything is rinsed with water a second time. It is estimated that approximately ten gallons of good quality water are needed for every one gallon of wine produced. Upon arriving at the winery, grapes are treated with fifty to seventy-five ppm of free sulfur dioxide. This process is called sulfating, and inhibits the unwanted microorganisms and wild yeast species on the grapes.

Grapes can simply be stepped on to free the juice, allowed to sit and they will become wine and later vinegar. Winemaking is the process of controlling the many variables that influence the taste of the wine to get the desired results. Grapes are fed into a corkscrew-shaped auger where they are first crushed, then if desired, de-stemmed. Stems exit at the end while juice, skins, and seeds exit the bottom. At this stage, red winemaking diverges from white winemaking. All grape juice is white.

It's the skin that imparts color to wine. Red wine is made from the pulpy juice, or must, of red or black grapes that undergo fermentation together with the grape skins. In addition to color, most flavor components of red wine are in the skin of the grape. White wine is made by fermenting juice that is made by pressing crushed grapes to extract a juice but the skins are removed and play no further role.

Occasionally white wine is made from red grapes. This entails extracting the juice with minimal contact with the red grapes' skins. Rosé wines are either made from red grapes where the juice is allowed to stay in contact with the dark skins long enough to pick up a pinkish color or by blending red wine and white wine. White Zinfandel is an example of a rosé wine made from black grapes. It is essentially a varietal rosé. White and rosé wines extract little of the tannins contained in the skins. Tannin is a naturally occurring organic chemical found in plants, seeds, wood, leaves, and fruit skins. Grape tannin, most commonly found in red wine, adds bitterness and astringency as well as complexity to wine.

To start primary fermentation, the juice is transferred to vats and yeast is added to the pulpy juice for red wine or juice for white wine. During this fermentation, which often takes between two and four weeks, the yeast converts most of the sugars in the grape juice into ethanol alcohol and carbon dioxide. The carbon dioxide is lost to the atmosphere. After the primary fermentation of red grapes the free run wine is pumped off into tanks and the skins are pressed to extract the remaining juice and wine. The press wine is blended with the free run wine at the wine maker's discretion. The wine is kept warm and the remaining sugars are converted into alcohol and carbon dioxide. The alcohol content of both white and red table wines and Champagne is ten to fourteen percent. Dessert wines are higher.

White wine is fermented similarly, but there are no skins. After fermentation, white wine goes through cold stabilization. This process requires the wine to drop almost to freezing to precipitate out the tartaric crystals that can form. The crystals are harmless, but this process can improve wine flavor. It also keeps consumers from getting nervous if they see crystals in their wine bottle.

The next process in the making of both red and white wine is secondary fermentation. This is a bacterial fermentation that converts sharp malic acid to mild lactic acid. This process decreases the acid in the wine and softens its taste. The tannic nature of high quality red wines is an important winemaking consideration. As the must is exposed to prolonged periods of skin contact, called maceration, more tannins are extracted from the skin and will be present in the resulting wine. If winemakers choose not to shorten the period of maceration, in favor of maximizing color and flavor concentrations, there are some methods that they can use to soften tannin levels. A common method is oak aging, which can mellow the harsh grape tannins as well as introduce softer 'wood tannins.' Fining agents can also reduce tannins.

In winemaking, fining is the process where a substance, called a fining agent, is added to the wine to create an absorbent, enzymatic, or ionic bond with the suspended particles. This makes them larger molecules that can precipitate out of the wine easier and quicker. Unlike filtration, which can only remove particles, such as dead yeast cells and grape fragments, fining is effective in removing soluble substances such as tannins, coloring phenols and proteins. Given enough time in a stable environment, many of these suspended particles would gradually precipitate out on their own. The use of fining agents speeds up the process at a lower cost. White wines are fined to remove particles that may cause the wine to brown or lose color as well as removing heat-unstable proteins that could cause the wine to appear hazy or cloudy should it be exposed to high temperatures after bottling. Red wines are fined for the same reasons but also for the added benefit of reducing the amount of bitter, astringent tannins which makes these wines smoother and more approachable sooner after bottling and release. Commonly used fining agents are gelatin and egg whites. They are positively charged proteins that are naturally attracted to the negatively charged tannin molecules. These fining agents will bond with some of the tannins and be removed from the wine during filtration.

Aging improves the flavor of the best wines. As wine rests in an oak barrel it goes through subtle chemical changes, resulting in greater complexity and a softening of the harsh tannins and flavors present at the end of fermentation. Aging in an oak barrel does three things: It allows a very slow introduction of oxygen into the wine, but not at levels that would cause oxidation or spoilage, which acts as a softening agent upon the tannins in the wine; it allows a small level of evaporation, which concentrates the wine's flavor and aroma compounds; and it imparts the character of the oak into the wine.

Wines that are higher in acidity and tannins benefit from longer aging in oak than wines that are not. Most red wines achieve all of the benefits of oak aging in one to two years. But some of the better ones continue to improve in oak for up to ten years. The only white varieties that improve with age are Chardonnay and Sauvignon Blanc and they are seldom barrel aged for more than a year. To help determine how long a wine should be aged in oak, winemakers use an instrument called a *wine thief* to taste the wine periodically during the aging process. It is a glass pipette, or tube, about eighteen inches long. The stopper on the side of the wine barrel is removed and the pipette is inserted into the wine in the barrel, where the part of the pipette in the wine fills. Then a thumb is placed over the end of the pipette, and the pipette, containing the wine, is withdrawn from the barrel. The wine in the pipette is then transferred to a wineglass by removing the thumb from the end of the pipette, and the wine is smelled and tasted.

Wine must be settled or clarified and adjustments made prior to filtration and bottling. It is then aged in the bottle. Bottle aging continues to soften the tannins and the result, after a long enough time, is a wine with a blend of the fruitiness of the grape, the oak from the barrel, and the mellowed tannins. A heavy, robust red wine that has been aged in oak for two years may continue to improve in the bottle for another ten to twenty years. Most red wines that are aged, though, will be aged in oak for about a year and improve in the bottle for up to five years. Most white wines that are aged in oak improve with age for three to five years in the bottle."

The total time that wins are aged in both oak barrels and the bottle can vary from a few months for simpler white wines to over twenty years for top red wines.

However, only about ten percent of red wines and five percent of white wines will improve enough with age to make drinking more enjoyable after five years of aging than after one year of aging.

Many wines of comparable quality are produced using different approaches to their production than just described. Quality is dictated by the attributes of the grapes and not necessarily the steps taken during winemaking. Numerous variations on the procedures just described exist. These variations constitute a winemaker's style. If five pieces of beautiful raw silk were given to each of five clothing designers, each would make a different dress from exactly the same material. But each would reflect the dressmaker's artistic talent. The winemaker is the same, and each will style their wines according to their artistic talent."

Red wines should be served at sixty-five to seventy degrees. Depending on the quality of the grape, reds should be allowed to breath after opening for ten minutes to an hour and whites from no time to about five minutes, to let off-odors dissipate. Red wines that have been aged for years may require decanting. This process entails slowly pouring the wine from its bottle into another glass container while holding a light or candle under the neck of the bottle to ensure none of the sediment gets into the decanted wine. Because they do not improve with aging beyond a few years, this isn't required for white wines. White wines should be served cold, at about forty to forty-five degrees. Chill by putting them in a bucket of ice and water for twenty minutes or in the refrigerator for one to two hours. Never chill them in the freezer because this will destroy delicate flavors.

The taste of wine is usually described by comparing it to fruits or other things. For reds, many describe them as tasting similar to black currants, black cherries, plums, or bell peppers. And for quality reds, such as Cabernet Sauvignon and Pinot Noir, there will be the taste of oak because of oak aging. For whites, its apples, pears, figs, grapefruit, pineapple, or in some cases flowery or floral, particularly for Gewurztraminer. For quality whites, such as Chardonnay, there will also be oakiness. The less sweet a wine is, the more these various types of flavors can be detected.

There are three methods used to make Champagne: *méthode Champenoise,* the transfer method, and the charmat bulk process. With *méthode Champenoise,* after primary fermentation and bottling, a second alcoholic fermentation occurs in the bottle. This second fermentation, which gives Champagne its carbonation from carbon dioxide, is induced by adding several grams of yeast and several grams of rock sugar. At this time, the Champagne bottle is capped with a crown cap. After aging a minimum of from one-and-a-half to three years, the residual yeast sediment, called lees, must be consolidated for removal. The bottles undergo a process known as riddling. In this stage, the bottles are placed on special racks at a forty-five degree angle with the cork pointed down. Every few days the bottles are given a slight shake and turn and dropped back into the racks. Eventually the angle is increased. The drop back into the rack causes a slight tap, pushing sediments toward the neck of the bottle. In about six to eight weeks the position of the bottle is pointed straight down with sediment in the neck of the bottle. The neck is then frozen, and the cap

19

removed. The pressure in the bottle forces out the lees, and the bottle is quickly corked to maintain the carbon dioxide in solution. This is the most expensive method of making Champagne.

After fermentation in a tank, the transfer method entails transferring the Champagne into bottles for secondary fermentation. When this is complete, it is transferred to a tank, filtered and bottled. This method allows for complexity to be built into the Champagne, but also gives scope for blending options after the Champagne has gone into the bottle. The cost of the transfer method is between *méthode Champenoise* and the third method, the charmat bulk process. In the charmat bulk process, the wine undergoes secondary fermentation in stainless steel tanks, then is bottled under pressure. this is the lowest-cost method of the three.

Styles of Champagne are from very dry to sweet. Their color ranges from white to pink to deep red, depending on the grape variety used. Champagnes require no breathing time and do not improve with age. They should not be stored for more than two years. They should be chilled in the refrigerator for two hours or in a bucket of ice and water for twenty to thirty minutes and served at forty to forty-five degrees, the same as white wine.

Dessert wines are sweet wines typically served with dessert, although they can be enjoyed alone as well as with fruit or bakery sweets. There are three types, Sherries, ports and late harvest wines. They contain high levels of sugar and are fourteen to twenty percent alcohol. They are made by ensuring that some residual sugar remains after fermentation is completed. This can be done by harvesting late, making late harvest wine, freezing the grapes to concentrate the sugar, also called ice wine, or adding alcohol, called fortification, before fermentation is completed. For example, wine spirits in the form of high proof brandy is added when making Sherry and port. In other cases the winemaker may choose to hold back some of the sweet grape juice and add it to the wine after the fermentation is done, a technique known as süssreserve.

Sherry is made from white grapes. Before the fermentation process is complete it is fortified with grape brandy, called wine spirits, to increase the alcohol level, then baked at one hundred thirty-five degrees for ten to fifteen weeks. This makes Cream Sherry. If the wine is allowed to complete fermentation and go completely dry before fortification it is a dry Sherry. Some Sherries may be oak-aged for twenty years or more. Sherry has a nutty-like taste.

Port is made from red grapes and is not baked. They are always made sweet. There are two kinds: tawny which is deep red to purple in color, and ruby, which is light red. Some tawny ports may be oak-aged for twenty years or longer. Ruby ports are light and do not improve with aging. Ports are often said to taste like raisins. Some of the most popular dessert wines are made from moldy grapes. But not just any mold. The mold is called Botrytis cinerea or noble rot. It sucks water out of the grape while imparting flavors of honey and apricot to the future wine. It typically occurs in over-ripe grapes left past normal harvest, usually into November. The weather conditions to produce noble rot occur only a few years out of ten. Many wines made in this way are called Thanksgiving harvest wines, and many are made from the Johannesburg Riesling variety of grape.

They are deep gold in color, complex in nature and are often described as tasting like apricots or peaches. Late harvest dessert wines improve with age up to and sometimes beyond ten years.

Sherry and port should be served at sixty-five to seventy degrees like red wines. Late harvest wines should be served at fifty-five to sixty degrees. Chill in a bucket of ice and water for ten to fifteen minutes or in the refrigerator for an hour. Dessert wines should be allowed to breathe for ten to fifteen minutes.

The main by-product from making wine is pomace, which is the pressed grape skins and seeds. It is sold as cattle feed. High proof made from wine stock is brandy, usually made from bad wines that are distilled into ethyl alcohol and sold to industrial users. Brandy is made by distilling and then barrel aging good wines. Wine vinegar is made from the fermentation of ethanol produced from wine by acetic acid bacteria. The process usually takes from several weeks to several months. A faster method entails adding a bacterial culture to the source liquid before adding air using a pump system or a turbine to promote oxygenation to speed fermentation. This process produces vinegar in one to three days.

The label on a bottle of table or dessert wine contains important information about that wine. It will of course have the name of the winery that's selling the wine; the wine class, which is the variety of grape it was made from if it is a varietal wine, or the name Burgundy, Chablis, or Bordeaux if it's a generic wine; its appellation, which is the country, state, county, and/or viticultural region where it was made; date of vintage; alcohol content; quantity of contents, such as seven hundred fifty milliliters; and the term 'Reserve' may be used to designate a special bottling or limited production. Finally there will be terms that tell you how it was made. 'Estate Bottled' means that one hundred percent of the wine was made from grapes grown in vineyards owned and managed by the named winery. 'Produced and Bottled by' means the named winery purchased, crushed, and fermented seventy-five percent or more of the grapes and aged and bottled the wine. 'Vinted and Bottled by' or 'Made and Bottled by' means that for seventy-six to ninety percent of the wine in that bottle, the named winery bought bulk wines made by another winery and aged, blended, and bottled them. 'Cellared and Bottled by' means the wines were produced by another winery and aged, bottled and marketed by the named winery. 'Bottled by' means the named winery only bottled and marketed the wine. For Champagne, the method used to make it will appear on the label along with the same information on wine labels.

Tasting Wines

It goes without saying that wine is an acquired taste. The more a person knows about a subject, the more they enjoy it, whether it's art, music, literature – or wine.

There are four major components that make up the taste of a wine. These are alcohol, acids, tannins and sugars. The major alcohol in wine is ethanol, the same as in beer, or distilled spirits like scotch and vodka, although obviously not nearly as much as in distilled spirits. Acids give wine longevity, balance and crispness. Chemical pH, or level of acidity, in wine affects a wine's color, taste, flavor and long-term stability. Tannins are present in all wines, but most notably in red wines. They come from the skins, stems and seeds of the grapes during fermentation, and also from oak barrels in which the wine is aged. Tannins are important in extending the life of wines, and supply a harsh, dry taste characteristic often described as puckery or astringent. This quality is reduced as a wine ages, giving it a mellow taste. Sugars are also present in all wines, and provide a detectable sweetness when they exceed one-half percent. When a wine is described as completely, or bone dry, the sweetness is undetectable.

The five key stages to wine tasting are those that make up sensory perception. These are color and clarity, the aroma of the wine in the glass, taste, the 'in-mouth' sensations, or mouth feel, and the finish, or after-taste. These five stages are combined in order to establish the following properties of a wine: complexity and character, potential or suitability for aging or drinking, and possible faults.

A wine's overall quality assessment, based on this examination, follows further careful description and comparison with recognized standards, both with respect to other wines in its price range and according to known factors pertaining to the region or vintage; if it is typical of the region or diverges in style; if it uses certain wine-making techniques, such as barrel fermentation or malolactic fermentation, or any other remarkable or unusual characteristics. Malolactic fermentation is a process in which tart-tasting malic acid naturally present in grapes is converted to softer-tasting lactic acid.

Whereas wines are regularly tasted in isolation, a wine's quality assessment is more objective when performed alongside several other wines, in what are known as tasting 'flights.' Wines may be deliberately selected for their vintage, which is horizontal tasting, or from a single winery, which is vertical tasting, to better compare vineyard and vintages, respectively. Alternatively, in order to promote an unbiased analysis, bottles and even glasses may be disguised in a 'blind' tasting, to rule out any prejudicial awareness of either vintage or winery.

To ensure impartial judgment of a wine, it should be served *blind* — that is, without the taster having seen the label or bottle shape. Blind tasting may also involve serving the wine from a black wineglass to mask the color of the wine. A taster can be prejudiced by knowing details of a wine, such as geographic origin, the winery that made it, price, reputation, color, or other considerations. Scientific research has long demonstrated the power of suggestion in perception as well as the strong effects of expectancies. For example, people expect more expensive wine to have more desirable characteristics than less expensive wine.

When given wine that they are falsely told is expensive they virtually always report it tastes better than the very same wine when they are told that it is inexpensive. French researcher Frédéric Brochet submitted a mid-range Bordeaux in two different bottles, one labeled as a cheap table wine, the other bearing a grand cru etiquette. Tasters described the supposed grand cru as 'woody, complex, and round' and the supposed cheap wine as 'short, light, and faulty.' Similarly, people have expectations about wines because of their geographic origin, producer, vintage, color, and many other factors. For example, when Brochet served a white wine he received all the usual descriptions: 'fresh, dry, honeyed, lively.' Later he served the same wine dyed red and received the usual red terms: 'intense, spicy, supple, deep.'

Vertical and horizontal wine tastings are wine tasting events that are arranged to highlight differences between similar wines," Alexis began after lunch. "In a vertical tasting, different vintages of the same wine type from the same winery are tasted. This emphasizes differences between various vintages. In a horizontal tasting, the wines are all from the same vintage but are from different wineries. Keeping wine variety or type and wine region the same helps emphasize differences in winery styles.

Tasting flight is a term used by wine tasters to describe a selection of wines, usually between three and eight glasses, but sometimes as many as fifty, presented for the purpose of sampling and comparison. A tasting note refers to a taster's written testimony about the aroma, taste identification, acidity, structure, texture, and balance of a wine. The temperature that a wine is served at can greatly affect the way it tastes and smells. Lower temperatures will emphasize acidity and tannins while muting the aromatics. Higher temperatures will minimize acidity and tannins while increasing the aromatics. General rules of thumb are that white wines and Champagnes should be served at forty to fifty degrees Fahrenheit, and red wines at sixty to seventy degrees.

The shape of a wineglass can have a subtle impact on the perception of wine, especially its bouquet. Typically, the ideal shape is considered to be wider toward the bottom, with a narrower aperture at the top, or tulip or egg shaped. Glasses that are widest at the top are considered the least ideal. Many wine tastings use glasses that are egg-shaped. Interestingly, the effect of glass shape does not appear to be related to whether the glass is pleasing to look at.

There are five basic steps in tasting wine: color, swirl, smell, taste, and savor. These are also known as the 'five S' steps for see, swirl, sniff, sip, and savor. During this process, a taster must look for clarity, varietal character, integration, expressiveness, complexity, and connectedness. Judging color is the first step in tasting wine. Without having tasted the wines, one does not know if, for example, a white is heavy or light. Before taking a sip, the taster tries to determine the order in which the wines should be assessed by appearance and nose alone. Heavy wines will be deeper in color and generally more intense on the nose. Sweeter wines, being denser, will leave thick, viscous streaks, called legs or fingers, down the inside of the glass when swirled. The wine should be bright and clear, with no particles in it. A wine's color is better judged by putting it against a white background. The wineglass is put at an angle in order to see the colors. Colors can give the taster clues to the grape variety, and whether the wine was aged in wood.

Varietal character describes how much a wine presents its inherent grape aromas. A wine taster also looks for integration, which is a state in which none of the components of the wine, acid, tannin, alcohol, is out of balance with the other components. When a wine is well balanced, the wine is said to have achieved a harmonious fusion. Another important quality of the wine to look for is its expressiveness. Expressiveness is the quality the wine possesses when its aromas and flavors are well-defined and clearly projected. The complexity of the wine is affected by many factors, one of which may be the multiplicity of its flavors. The connectedness of the wine, a rather abstract and difficult to ascertain quality, describes the bond between the wine and its land of origin, or terroir.

A wine's quality can be judged by its bouquet and taste. The bouquet is the total aromatic experience of the wine. Assessing a wine's bouquet can also reveal faults such as cork taint, oxidation due to age, overexposure to oxygen, or lack of preservatives and wild yeast contamination due to Brettanomyces or acetobacter yeasts. Although low levels of Brettanomyces aromatic characteristics can be a positive attribute, giving the wine a distinctive character, generally it is considered a wine spoilage yeast. The bouquet of wine is best revealed by gently swirling the wine in a wineglass to expose it to more oxygen and release more aromatic etheric, ester, and aldehyde molecules that comprise the essential components of a wine's bouquet. Sparkling wine should not be swirled to the point of releasing bubbles.

Pausing to experience a wine's bouquet aids the wine taster in anticipating the wine's flavors. The 'nose' of a wine, its bouquet or aroma, is the major determinate of perceived flavor in the mouth. Once inside the mouth, the aromatics are further liberated by exposure to body heat, and transferred retro-nasally to the olfactory receptor site. It is here that the complex taste experience characteristic of a wine actually commences.

Thoroughly tasting a wine involves perception of its array of taste and mouth feel attributes, which involve the combination of textures, flavors, weight, and overall structure. Following appreciation of its olfactory characteristics, the wine taster savors a wine by holding it in the mouth for a few seconds to saturate the taste buds. By pursing one's lips and breathing through that small opening oxygen will pass over the wine and release even more esters. When the wine is allowed to pass slowly through the mouth it presents the connoisseur with the fullest gustatory profile available to the human palate.

The acts of pausing and focusing through each step distinguish wine tasting from simple quaffing. Through this process, the full array of aromatic molecules is captured and interpreted by approximately fifteen million olfactory receptors, comprising a few hundred olfactory receptor classes. When tasting several wines in succession, however, key aspects of this fuller experience, length and finish, or aftertaste, must necessarily be sacrificed through expectoration.

Although taste qualities are known to be widely distributed throughout the oral cavity, the concept of an anatomical 'tongue map' yet persists in the wine tasting arena, in which different tastes are believed to map to different areas of the tongue. A widely accepted example is the misperception that the tip of the tongue uniquely tells how sweet a wine is and the upper edges tell its acidity.

As part of the tasting process, and as a way of comparing the merits of the various wines, wines are given scores according to a relatively set system. This may be either by explicitly weighting different aspects, or by global judgment, although the same aspects would be considered. These aspects are one, the appearance of the wine, two, the nose or smell, three, the palate or taste, and four, the overall effect of these three aspects. Different systems weight these differently. That is, appearance fifteen percent, nose thirty- five percent, palate fifty percent. Typically, no modern wine would score less than half on any scale, which would effectively indicate an obvious fault. It is more common for wines to be scored out of twenty, including half marks, in Europe and parts of Australasia, and out of one-hundred in the United States. However, different critics tend to have their own preferred system, and some grades are also given out of five, again with half marks.

Because intoxication can affect the consumer's judgment, wine tasters generally spit the wine out after they have assessed its quality at formal tastings, where dozens of wines may be assessed. However, since wine is absorbed through the skin inside the mouth, tasting from twenty to twenty-five samplings can still produce an intoxicating effect, depending on the alcoholic content of the wine.

Generic wines are a blend of a number of grape varieties, and can be divided into two classes: ordinary wines and premium wines. Ordinary wines may simply be called red table wine and white table wine, or they may carry the name of a grape production region in Europe. Thus, the reds may be called Burgundy, Bordeaux or Chianti, and the whites Chablis or Rhine wine. Ordinary generic wines are made from blends of lower-priced grapes. For reds these include Barbera, Carignane, Gamay Beaujolais, Petite Sirah, Ruby Cabernet, Grenach, and others. For whites, Burger, Chenin Blanc, Thompson seedless, French Colombard, Palomino, Sauvignon Blanc, Gray Riesling, Semillon, and others. Premium generics are made from higher quality grapes, and also carry the name of grape production regions in Europe. Again, Burgundy, Bordeaux, and Chianti for reds, and Chablis and Rhine wine for whites. Grapes used in premium Burgundy and Bordeaux include Cabernet Sauvignon, Merlot, Pinot Noir, Zinfandel and Petite Sirah. Grape varieties used in premium Chablis and Rhine wine include Chardonnay, Sauvignon Blanc, Chenin Blanc, Johannisberg Riesling, and Gewurztraminer. Prices for generic wines cover a very wide range, from $3 - $7 for an ordinary wine, $10 to $15 for premium whites and reds, to over a hundred dollars for the highest quality aged Burgundy and Bordeaux, equal to prices for the highest quality red varietals.

Premium generics can be either dry, with a very clean, crisp taste, or less dry, with detectable sweetness from residual sugar. Residual sugar is any natural grape sugars left over after fermentation ceases. Dry wines usually have less than 0.3 percent residual sugar, medium wines one to three percent, and sweet wines have more than three percent residual sugar.

The highest quality premium generics are dry, full bodied, and intense, with an expansive bouquet. Less experienced wine drinkers often believe that ordinary generic wines are inferior, and only drink varietals or premium generics, but that's not necessarily true. We don't have filet mignon or roast duck every night. A nice Burgundy or red table wine can go well with a hamburger or ham sandwich, as can a Chablis with a turkey sandwich or grilled chicken salad. There is relative value in a $40 dollar bottle of wine and in a $10 dollar bottle of wine. Drink the ordinary generics to appreciate the premium generics and more complex varietals.

Rosé wines are made from red or black grapes, but left in contact with the skins for only a short time – a few hours. Otherwise, they are made like a white wine. They may be blends of several varieties, such as Zinfandel, Gamay Beaujolais, and Barbera, or made from only one variety, Zinfandel for example. Rosés are typically light, fruity, lively and delicate. Colors range from light pink to light red, and taste from very dry, to medium body, to sweet with residual sugar. They should be served chilled like a white wine. Two hours in the refrigerator or twenty minutes in a bucket of half ice and half water.

Champagne has the reputation of being the beverage of kings and queens, and for special occasions. In France, it is made from grapes grown in the Champagne region, while in the United States, it is called both Champagne and sparkling wine, and is made in New York state and California. It may be a blend, or made from a single variety of grape. Some Champagnes are made completely dry and some with residual sugar. However, extra dry refers to a Champagne that is slightly sweet. Pink Champagne is a rosé Champagne. Champagnes are made in a limitless range of styles, from dry to sweet, white to pink to deep red. Taste is light, fresh and fruity.

Dessert wines consist of Sherries, ports, and late harvest Riesling. Sherries are sweet or dry. If the wine is fermented until it is dry before adding wine spirits, it is a dry, or cocktail, Sherry. If fermentation is stopped while there is still sugar in the wine before adding wine spirits, it is a cream Sherry. Sherry may be an aperitif as well as a dessert wine. It is nutty in flavor and usually amber in color. The best Sherries are oak aged, which makes them brown in color.

Ports are always made sweet. They are produced from red or black grapes, and the style is fruity and mellow. Ports may be made from a blend of varieties, or from one variety. Tawny port may be aged in oak for five years or more, and bottled aged for ten years or longer. Some of the best tawny ports are over a hundred years old. Ruby port is light and fruity, and not aged. Late harvest Rieslings are deep gold in color, luscious and sweet. Taste is often compared to peaches, apricots and even honey. They improve with bottle aging for up to ten years.

Serve Sherries and ports at sixty-five degrees F., and late harvest Rieslings slightly colder – at fifty-five degrees.

If fifty wine experts were asked their opinion about Chardonnay, all would agree that it is the best quality white varietal. Chardonnay has a buttery character, rich and full-bodied, and is pale gold in color. It lends itself well to a variety of winemakers' styles. It's a work horse grape, but also a grape with finesse. You can make a delicate

Chardonnay, fresh, light, crisp, and fruity, or just the opposite, rich, oaky, complex, and powerful. It ages well in oak, which adds complexity. The best Chardonnays will be aged in oak for a year, and improve with age for up to another five to ten years in the bottle. Most however, do not improve in the bottle for more than three to five years. The taste of Chardonnay is often compared to herbs, lemons, apples, apricots and peaches, with a woody taste from oak aging. It is always dry.

Sauvignon Blanc, if aged in oak for up to a year, is a close second to Chardonnay. In fact, some feel that Sauvignon Blanc offers a formidable challenge to Chardonnay for white wine supremacy. Sauvignon Blanc is a very distinctive wine that is different from all others. It has a very intense, spicy flavor, herbal and fig-like. People either like it a lot, or not at all. It ranges from light yellow to medium gold, and after being aged in oak, improves with bottle aging for another five to ten years.

Johannisberg Riesling is the classic grape of Germany. It is perfumy and grapey in character. Styles range from slightly sweet, with one to two percent residual sugar because of the higher acidity of Johannisberg Riesling grapes, to fresh, fragrant and crisp, to dry. It is pale straw-colored, with a green tint. It is not aged in oak, and improves in the bottle for up to five years.

Chenin Blanc is a good introduction to white varietals, or to varietal wines for new wine drinkers. It is simple, soft, and fruity, and does not have the intensity of character of Chardonnay or Sauvignon Blanc. It is a very light straw color. Chenin Blanc does not improve with age, and is best if consumed within four years of when it was made.

Gewürztraminer has a unique, floral, perfumy character. Many say that it tastes like a rose smells. Its flavor is intense, very fruity and spicy. A good wine for new wine drinkers. Styles range from dry to sweet with one to two percent residual sugar. It is light straw-colored. Gewürztraminer is not oak aged, and improves in the bottle for up to five years.

Cabernet Sauvignon is considered the king of the red wines. It is also the most elegant of the red wines, and is the most consistently well-made red varietal. Cabernet Sauvignons are among the world's best wines. The grapes need a cool climate to keep the acid high enough. They are small and berry-sized, which results in more skin per gallon, and more color and flavor. Its intense, powerful character lends itself to many styles. The amount of tannin and the ratio of fruit to wood taste are the biggest variables in style. Cabernet Sauvignon has a wide variety of aromatic descriptions. From spicy, fruity and plumy, to herbaceous and bell peppery. Almost always made dry, its complexity and elegance of flavors is what makes it so desirable. When young, Cabernet Sauvignon is harsh and needs at least five to eight years of aging. Lighter styles age gracefully up to ten years, while heavier, outstanding vintages will improve up to fifty years. Cabernet Sauvignon needs to breathe at least fifteen minutes, with the more complex wines requiring up to an hour of breathing time.

Lighter in color and taste than Cabernet Sauvignon, Pinot Noir is considered the queen of red wines, second only to Cabernet Sauvignon. Pinot Noir is velvety in mouth feel, and chemically different in color than any other red wine. Its taste is minty, toasty, oaky, and earthy. It is soft in body and very dry, but with age, develops a seemingly sweet quality. It is best if consumed five to ten years after it is made and needs fifteen minutes breathing time. It is difficult to make well. Many experts believe that a winemaker's skill can be determined by how well they make Pinot Noir.

Merlot is primarily a blending grape, but also makes a good varietal. It is moderate, soft, and mild, with a light, fruity flavor. Its taste is like ripe cherries or plums. Aromas are cherry fruitiness, herbal tea, and orange rind. The aging time for Merlot is about half that for Cabernet Sauvignon. It needs fifteen minutes breathing time.

Zinfandel is an extremely versatile grape. It makes good red wines as well as rosés, often called white Zinfandel. A good port can also be made from the late harvest of Zinfandel grapes. Zinfandel has a great deal of berry-like character. It has a full taste, well balanced, and not high in acid, so it can be soft. It has a rich, berry fruit taste, with a peppery quality. Its taste is often compared to raspberries, blackberries, cranberries and boysenberries. Zinfandel is medium red to deep purple in color. As a table wine, it does not improve with age, but as late harvest desert wine, it can improve for ten years or more. It needs only about ten minutes breathing time.

Petite Sirah is the last of the varietals we will examine. It is primarily used as a blending grape for body and color, but is also made into a varietal. Very dark in color, it is almost black like India ink. It is direct, simple, and full-bodied, with a narrow range of styles. Petite Sirah has strong tannins, and thus an astringent taste, but it develops well from aging. It will benefit from three to six years of bottle aging, although some may continue to improve for up to ten years. It is usually too strong to drink without food, such as lamb shank, prime rib, aged cheeses, and other strong foods. It needs 15 minutes to an hour of breathing time.

Wine is good as an aperitif, or cocktail, without food, and certainly with food. The best practice is to eat the foods you like with the wines you like. However, a general guideline is to match complex wines that have a more robust flavor with heavier more powerful foods, and softer, simpler wines with lighter foods. Thus a Cabernet Sauvignon or very high quality Bordeaux would go well with lamb, beef, venison, Italian sausage, and so on, while foods that would go well with Chenin Blanc or Chablis would include fish, shellfish, poultry, and salads. An example of foods that would go well with wines between these two extremes, such as Chardonnay, Johannisberg Riesling, Pinot Noir, and Zinfandel would be roast pork, duck, veal, tuna salad, pasta, and quail.

Corkscrews date back to the sixteenth century, and there are many different kinds. A basic corkscrew consists of a pointed metal spiral, called a helix, attached to a handle, which is a horizontal bar of wood. The user grips the handle and screws the metal point into the cork. Its point should puncture the cork with a small hole and penetrate smoothly, without damaging a lot of cork tissue. Once the helix is firmly embedded into the cork, a vertical pull on the corkscrew extracts the cork from the bottle. The wing-type has metal levers or wings on each side of the helix. As the helix is twisted into the cork, the wings are raised. Once the helix is embedded in the cork, pushing down the wings pulls the cork out of the bottle in one smooth motion. The most common design has a rack and pinion connecting the levers to the body. A sommelier knife, or waiter's friend, is a corkscrew in a folding body similar to a pocket knife. An arm extends to brace against the lip of the bottle for leverage when removing the cork. A small hinged knife blade is housed in the handle end to be used in cutting the foil wrapping the neck of many wine bottles. A corkscrew of this type is less intuitive to use, and requires more skill in order to be used without damaging the cork, but can be used more quickly and with more show than a wing-type corkscrew.

The twin prong cork puller can extract a cork without damaging it, to allow for sampling the wine before re-inserting the cork. The cork is removed by first inserting the longer prong between the cork and neck of the bottle, and pushing it down until the shorter prong is inserted between the cork and bottle neck on the other side. The device is then rocked first on the side of one prong, then on the side of the other prong, while pushing down on it until the prongs are inserted the length of the cork. The cork is then twisted out of the bottle. The twin prong cork puller is also known as the butler's friend, because it enables wine to be removed from its bottle and replaced with a less expensive wine without knowing the wine bottle was opened. Another very good corkscrew is the screw pull developed by Herbert Allen. The screw pull has a Teflon-coated helix, which enables it to more easily penetrate the cork without damaging much cork tissue. It has plastic grips on each side of the helix. When removing the cork, the grips are held firmly against the neck of the wine bottle while the helix is screwed into the cork. As it penetrates the cork, the cork is pulled out of the bottle.

In opening a bottle of Champagne, safety is the key because there are about six atmospheres of pressure in the bottle. You don't want the cork exploding out of the bottle because it could break something or hurt someone, and you don't want Champagne foaming out of the bottle either because you want to drink it instead of lose it. Peel off the part of the foil that covers the top inch of the bottle. Then, holding your thumb firmly on the top of the cork, twist the loop on the wire hood to loosen it, and lift it off. Next, hold the bottle at a forty-five degree angle and, grasping the cork with your hand, turn the bottle while pulling upward on the cork until it comes out. Champagne should be served in a tall, narrow glass flute, not the bird bath-type glasses that it is often served in at parties. The flute directs the bouquet to the top of the glass where it can be enjoyed instead of around the sides where it is lost, like the bird bath-type glass does.

When a waiter brings you the wine you have ordered in a restaurant, the waiter will show you the label prior to opening the wine. Be sure it is the wine you ordered. After removing the cork, he or she will show it to you. Squeeze it to be sure it is pliable. If it is hard, split, or cracked, and not pliable, it could have dried out when the wine was stored and let oxygen into the wine, which oxidizes and ruins it. Wine should always be stored on its side, to keep the cork from drying out. Once the wine has been allowed to breathe, if appropriate for the wine you ordered to let any off-odors dissipate, the waiter will pour a small amount of the wine in a glass for you. Swirl the wine in the glass and smell it, then taste it. If it is bad, it will have a heavy, grassy, musty smell and taste, or a sour smell and taste like vinegar. This is rare, but if the wine is bad, refuse to pay for it.

Some things are good for their simplicity — a smoldering campfire, a tune you can whistle. Others reward deeper examination — an antique time-piece, a perfectly executed triple axel in figure skating, and, yes, a fine wine. Passionate craftsmen, generations of tradition and glances toward future possibilities all come together in a glass of wine. But it starts with opening a bottle (*Wine Spectator*).

Also By Robert Allen Morris

Available at www.amazon.com in paperback or on Kindle

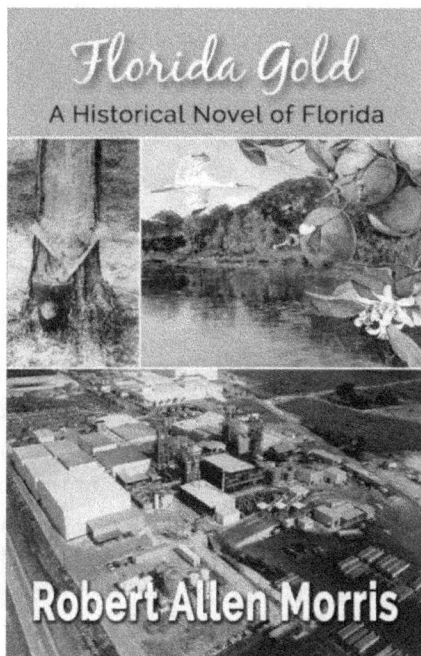

Florida Gold
A Historical Novel of Florida
Robert Allen Morris

It's 1988, and Jack Thomas, the 73-year-old CEO of Tropical Juices, finally about to retire, reflects upon his life. The story quickly shifts back to Jack's birth in 1915 in a turpentine-making camp in rural Florida. The child of 15-year-old Irma Sue, who had been seduced by the son of a local moonshiner, Jack is to be raised as her brother by her parents, Pete and Margaret. Pete, however, is soon killed in a horse-riding accident. Irma Sue and Margaret move to Mobile, Alabama, hoping to earn enough money to bring Jack, left behind with friends, into a new home. Fortune smiles upon the attractive women, both marrying advantageously. The family reunites briefly before Jack is snatched to work the fields at one of Florida's illegal child labor camps. With the assistance of local Native Americans, Jack escapes from the camp as a teenager. He returns to Mobile, learns of further family catastrophe, then helps the feds bust up the camps. With seed money from a surprising source, Jack starts an orange-juice business in Florida, serves with distinction in World War II and continually expands his enterprise. By novel's end, he heads a multibillion-dollar company, although still more family losses make success bittersweet. Morris, an agricultural economist with over 30 years of experience in the citrus industry, brings plenty of insider knowledge and passion to this fictional work, managing to make sequences featuring the main character, Jack Thomas' savvy with concentrate, cartons that don't leak, and other innovations quite engaging. His narrative gets a bit overripe at times, given the seemingly never-ending and near-superhuman heroics of his main character as well as a rather melodramatic string of family tragedies. Still, this novel is ultimately highly entertaining, and a surprisingly juicy account about a key segment of commerce in the Sunshine State. --- *Kirkus Reviews*

Florida Gold by Robert Allen Morris was one of those 'wow factor' books. An amazingly told story, with real feeling put into the words. It's an unforgettable story, one that I could read over again and still   take something new away from it. The characters are real and fit the story, the plot was well thought out and researched, and the whole book flows properly. Robert Morris is clearly a natural born storyteller and I would love to read more from him. – *Readers' Favorite*

Florida Gold was inducted into the Florida Citrus Archives on September 24, 2014. The event was hosted by the Lawton Chiles Center for Florida History on the Campus of Florida Southern College in Lakeland, Florida.

The Wine Queen

Love, Romance, and A Woman's Quest For Success In The California Wine Industry

Robert Allen Morris

Ann Robinson is orphaned at the age of eight and sent to live with her Uncle Dave and mean-spirited, manipulative Aunt Harriett. Ann is smart, works hard in school, and goes to college. She graduates at the top of her class with a degree in economics, and accepts a job as a sales manager. When she sees Ray Collins presenting a paper at professional meetings, she becomes infatuated with him. But she learns that he's married with a family, although his marriage is troubled. Ann can't get Ray off of her mind, and ultimately decides that if she can't have Ray, then she'll never get married. She goes back to school, gets her master's degree, and climbs the corporate ladder at the Global Soft Drink Company. Ray's marriage finally ends, and when he and Ann go on their first date, they are powerfully attracted to each other. They subsequently fall deeply in love, have an incredibly romantic courtship, and get married. Ann is devastated when their marriage comes to an unexpected and abrupt end. She accepts a position as the chief financial officer for the Columbia Creek Winery, and moves to Napa, California. With the help of an equity investment from the Global Soft Drink Company, Ann buys the winery. She subsequently makes wines and develops new wine blends that become very popular and gain international recognition. Sales soar and she grows Columbia Creek Winery into the largest wine company in the world. But she never gives up on love and romance, as demonstrated by the surprising ending.

Reviewed by Valerie Rouse for Readers' Favorite

"The Wine Queen by Robert Allen Morris is a delightful story about a bright, educated young lady with good business acumen. It tells a tale about dedication. The main character, Ann Robinson, always committed herself to her goals and excelled. This is an admirable trait. Author Robert Morris did an excellent job developing the main character and displaying her inner strength and boldness. This feature is one which all readers should uphold. The tone is colloquial and quite easy to follow. I love the emphasis the author placed on the romance portion of the novel. This section was very intense emotionally and I was caught up in the rapture of the heated romance. I identified with Ann and felt that she deserved the attention and love being given. This indicates the creative genius of the author. I love the fact that the author chose to provide a little background on the upbringing of the main character. This allows the reader to understand her personality on a deeper level. The twist at the end was totally unexpected. It is not very realistic, but it is entertaining to read nevertheless. Overall, The Wine Queen is a good read, and I recommend it to all readers."
Readers' Favorite

About The Author

Robert Allen Morris is an agricultural economist with thirty-six years of experience in agribusiness. He spent most of his career working for large companies. These included Duda, a company with agricultural operations in Florida, Texas and California; The Coca-Cola Company; Tropicana Products; Cutrale, one of the world's largest citrus processors, growers and exporters, based in Araraquara, Brazil; and Prudential Agricultural Investments. In 2007, Allen joined the faculty of the University of Florida in the Food and Resource Economics Department of the Institute of Food and Agricultural Sciences, with responsibilities for both educational programs and research. In April, 2012, he resigned his faculty appointment and joined Blue Lake Citrus Products as Vice-President of Sales and Marketing. Blue Lake Citrus Products produces and markets the Noble brand of high-end specialty citrus juices as well as bulk citrus juices for other brands and labels. Allen has published more than thirty articles on agribusiness and has given numerous presentations world-wide. When he worked for The Coca-Cola Company in the 1980s, his responsibilities were in The Wine Spectrum, their wine subsidiary. The Wine Spectrum, which was comprised of The Taylor Wine company in New York State, and Taylor California Cellars, The Monterey Vineyards and Sterling Vineyards in California, was the second largest wine company in North America. While working there, he was sent to wine school, and taught the basics of viticulture, enology, and wine tasting, experiences that provided much of his background for writing this book. Allen currently resides with his wife, Kate, in Winter Haven, Florida, and can be reached at Allenmors@aol.com. Visit www.AllenMorrisOnline.com for more literary works by Allen.

www.ingramcontent.com/pod-product-compliance
Lightning Source LLC
Chambersburg PA
CBHW020528030426
42337CB00011B/576